GW01454292

Heinrich Heine
North Sea Poems

Selected, translated & introduced by
Richard Crockatt

Arc
PUBLICATIONS
2021

Published by Arc Publications,
Nanholme Mill, Shaw Wood Road
Todmorden OL14 6DA, UK
www.arcpublications.co.uk

978 1910345 75 7

Design by Tony Ward
Printed in the UK by ImprintDigital.com

Cover photograph by Julia Crockatt

For Philip and Ian Crockatt

ACKNOWLEDGEMENTS
The author would like to thank his brothers Philip and Ian,
and also Jennie Feldman, for reading the manuscript and for
their encouragement and support. He is grateful also to
Jean Boase-Beier for her detailed comments and
suggestions, which were invaluable. His thanks, as always, go
to Julia Crockatt for her unstinting support

Arc Chapbook Series
Series Editor: Tony Ward

CONTENTS

Introduction / 5

Heinrich Heine was born in Düsseldorf in 1797 and died in Paris in 1856, where for twenty-five years he had lived in exile from his native Germany. His move reflected his attraction to the revolutionary ideas of France and also the struggle for a writer of his political stripe to flourish in Germany. Known chiefly as a poet, he was also the author of numerous prose works, many of which expressed radical political views unacceptable to the German authorities. Much of his later poetry too was troubling to the German censor, not least his long satirical poems of the 1840s *Atta Troll: Ein Sommernachtstraum* (Atta Troll: A Midsummer Night's Dream) and *Deutschland: Ein Wintermärchen* (Germany: A Winter's Tale).

The young Heine was, however, predominantly a lyric poet. *Die Nordsee* (The North Sea) was the product of his early years when he was still living in Germany. The poems resulted from visits to the island of Norderney on the north German coast and were published in 1827 as part of the *Buch der Lieder* (Book of Songs). This was Heine's breakthrough publication which became not only his best-known book but the most popular of all German books of poetry. Translations of his poetry into numerous other languages ensured that, with the exception of Goethe, he would be the most widely read German poet outside Germany. Not least among the reasons for the popularity of the *Book of Songs* in Germany and elsewhere was that so many of his poems were set to music by, among others, Schubert, Mendelssohn and Schumann. There are around three thousand settings of his poems.

A vital clue to Heine's poetry is to be found in his relation to the Romantic movement. Much of his early lyric poetry lies squarely within the Romantic tradition of self-expression on the subjects of love, loss, and the beauty and terrors of nature. In this vein he wrote some of the most beautiful and haunting lyrics in the German language. Yet even in these early years there are hints of a powerful strain of irony and scepticism which in his later writings came to predominate. There are many poems in the *Book of Songs*, not least in the *North Sea* series, in which the bubble of Romantic expression is punctured by a deflationary and sometimes cruel sense of irony. Often the irony is at his own expense, suggesting a troubled soul for whom life presented pain and disappointment as well as moments of intense inspiration and pleasure. In the eyes of some this diminishes Heine's stature as a poet. He seemed uncomfortable with sustained expression of elevated feelings and beliefs, being too ready, so his critics say, to take the easy route of cutting down what he had built up. One eminent critic, referring specifically to the *North Sea* poems, deplored Heine's 'disunity of mood' which, he added, was 'detrimental to poetry'.

This is to take an excessively narrow view of Heine and of poetry more generally. For one thing, Romanticism was rarely expressed in a single register, any more than other literary traditions have been. Wit, irony, and humour abound in the writings of many Romantics which is what one would expect in a poetry based on the expression of self-consciousness which is always liable to spill over into ironic detachment or mockery, whether at one's own or others' expense. For another thing, since the time of the great modernist poets of the early twentieth century, we have become used to multiple voices and moods in the same poem and are less shocked by the spectre of a poet undercutting his/her imaginative projections.

Heine was, of course, far from being a modernist, even in anticipation. His poetry contains none of the formal experimentation one associates with modernist poetry. The "disunity" of tone and mood in Heine is, however, integral to his poetic personality; it was part of his psyche which he exploited poetically with great formal skill and which, for all its associations with Romanticism, has a peculiarly modern feel. In this regard, embedded as he was in his own time, Heine's poetry has the power to speak to us across time. His "disunity" expresses also a deep ambivalence about nature between the Romantic tendency to ascribe emotion to natural phenomena (the so-called "pathetic fallacy") and an awareness of the total indifference of nature to human feelings and thoughts. The *North Sea* poems are rich in reflections on this deeply human conflict. All of which is to suggest that if Heine's poetry was an expression of Romanticism, it was also a critique of it.

Heine's *North Sea* poems are unusual in two respects: firstly they are in free verse, unlike the bulk of his poetic output which was predominantly in rhymed quatrains; secondly, it is the first collection of sea poems in the German language. To call them sea poems, however, is somewhat misleading. The immediate setting of the *North Sea* poems is the sea-shore and the life of the people in the small fishing communities of the island of Norderney. But Heine was no documentary realist. What he sees is coloured by his varied emotions, including an appetite for humour and a certain innate gusto, but above all by his drive as a poet to give form and structure to his emotions. While the poems contain vivid descriptions of varied states of the sea and the shore, the sea in these poems is essentially a screen onto which Heine projected his imagination. Local characters and scenes feature in his poems as fleeting presences rather than filled-out portraits and descriptions. Furthermore, Heine's imagination was informed not only by the dilemmas of his own psyche but by a preoccupation with the gods of the classical world as well as – though to a lesser extent – Christianity and Nordic myths. In short, a mixture of registers is of the essence in Heine's poetry.

The *North Sea* is made up of two 'cycles', with twelve poems in the first and ten in the second. The selection offered here constitutes half of the total, predominantly

7

from the first cycle, with the aim of presenting not only the variety of moods and colours in Heine's poems but also a loose narrative which takes us from the shore, to scenes aboard ship, and the return to harbour, ending with a pastoral scene in which the sea has been truly left behind. While visiting Norderney, Heine was reading Johann Heinrich Voss's translation of the *Odyssey*, and several of the poems, not included here, address directly the life and influence of the gods of classical Greece. However, a mythic dimension is present in all the poems selected, and it seemed preferable to choose those poems in which the mythic strain is most fully integrated into the poetry. Selecting the poems on this basis serves also to bring out more strongly the narrative element in the sequence.

For the translator these poems seemingly present a gift by virtue of their freedom from the tight rhyme schemes which characterize much of the poetry in the *Book of Songs*. However, Heine's free verse is always rhythmically alert and carefully structured through repetition of words and phrases and by more or less subtle modulations of tone and expression. In that sense, Heine's *North Sea* poems are like the sea itself – apparently formless yet moving according to a myriad known forces and conditions, even if precise shapes and outcomes cannot be predicted. Heine was capable of considerable rhetorical flights as well as dramatic, even melodramatic, collisions of the real and the mythical. My aim has been to convey the *brio* in Heine's lines, the sense in which he pushes at limits, without losing the clarity and tightness of his observations of nature and human life. To read these poems is to take a journey with Heine through a borderland of the imagination where the sea meets the land and many surprising transformations take place.

Richard Crockatt

NORTH SEA POEMS

ABENDDÄMMERUNG

Am blassen Meeresstrande
Saß ich gedankenbekümmert und einsam.
Die Sonne neigte sich tiefer, und warf
Glührote Streifen auf das Wasser,
Und die weißen, weiten Wellen,
Von der Flut gedrängt,
Schäumten and rauschten näher und näher –
Ein seltsam Geräusch, ein Flüstern und Pfeifen,
Ein Lachen und Murmeln, Seufzen und Sausen,
Dazwischen ein wiegenliedheimliches Singen –
Mir war, als hört ich verschollne Sagen,
Uralte, liebliche Märchen,
Die ich einst, als Knabe,
Von Nachbarskindern vernahm,
Wenn wir am Sommerabend,
Auf den Treppensteinen der Haustür,
Zum stillen Erzählen niederkauerten,
Mit kleinen, horchenden Herzen
Und neugierklugen Augen;-
Während die großen Mädchen,
Neben duftenden Blumentöpfen,
Gegenüber am Fenster saßen,
Rosengesichter,
Lächelnd und mondbeglänzt.

DUSK

Dusk triggers memories of childhood and the wider imaginative world of myth and fable, setting the scene for the whole sequence in which myth and everyday reality intersect.

On the pale seashore
I sat alone with troubled thoughts.
The sun dropped lower and cast
Glowing red streaks on the water;
And the wide white waves,
Driven in by the flood,
Foamed and roared ever closer
With a curious hissing, whispering and whistling,
Laughing and murmuring, sighing and seething,
But through it all, the soothing sound of a lullaby –
Like an echo of long lost legends,
Ancient treasured tales
Which I heard as a boy
From the neighbours' children
When we sat on summer evenings
On the stone steps by the front door,
Squatting down to hear the stories,
With our tiny listening hearts
And bright eager eyes;--
While the older girls sat
Beside fragrant flower pots
Over by the window,
Their faces like roses,
Smiling and bathed in moonlight.

SONNENUNTERGANG

Die glühend rote Sonne steigt
Hinab ins weitaufschauernde,
Silbergraue Weltenmeer;
Luftgebilde, rosig angehaucht,
Wallen ihr nach; und gegenüber,
Aus herbstlich dämmernden Wolkenschleiern,
Ein traurig todblasses Antlitz,
Bricht hervor der Mond,
Und hinter ihm, Lichtfünkchen,
Nebelweit, schimmern die Sterne.

Einst am Himmel glänzten,
Eh'lich vereint,
Luna, die Göttin, und Sol, der Gott,
Und es wimmelten um sie her die Sterne,
Die kleinen, unschuldigen Kinder.

Die böse Zungen zischelten Zwiespalt,
Und es trennte sich feindlich
Das hohe, leuchtende Ehepaar.
Jetzt am Tage, in einsamer Pracht,
Ergeht sich dort oben der Sonnengott,
Ob seiner Herrlichkeit
Angebetet und vielbesungen
Von stolzen, glückgehärteten Menschen.
Aber des Nachts,
Am Himmel, wandelt Luna,
Die arme Mutter

SUNSET

Heine's preoccupation with Classical myths, in this instance Roman, colour his perception of nature. For Heine the story of Sol and Luna shows the lapse from an original unity and harmony in nature into its present fallen state, in effect a version of the Christian fall.

The glowing red sun sinks
Down to the heaving
Silver-grey ocean;
Airy rose-tinted images
Bubble up behind, while far opposite,
Through darkening veils of cloud,
The deathly pallor
Of the autumnal moon
Breaks forth,
And beyond, tiny sparks of light
In the misty distance –
The shimmering stars.

Once in the heavens,
Luna the goddess and Sol the god
Shone together,
Joined in marriage,
And round about them thronged the stars,
Their innocent little children.

But wicked tongues hissed discord,
And the exalted radiant pair
Parted in bitter enmity.

Now all day in lonely splendour
The sun god assumes his lordly place,
Idolized, and his praises sung
By proud mortals with hearts hardened by luck.
But at night, in the heavens
Wanders Luna,
The sorrowing mother,

Mit ihren verwaisten Sternenkindern,
Und sie glänzt in stiller Wehmut,
Und liebende Mädchen und sanfte Dichter
Weihen ihr Tränen und Lieder.
Die weiche Luna! Weiblich gesinnt,
Liebt sie noch immer den schönen Gemahl.
Gegen Abend, zitternd und bleich,
Lauscht sie hervor aus leichtem Gewölk,
Und schaut nach dem Scheidenden, schmerzlich,
Und möchte ihm ängstlich rufen: "Komm!
Komm! Die Kinder verlangen nach dir – "
Aber der trotzige Sonnengott,
Bei dem Anblick der Gattin erglüht er
In doppeltem Purpur,
Vor Zorn und Schmerz,
Und unerbittlich eilt er hinab
In sein flutenkaltes Witwerbett.

Böse, zischelnde Zungen
Brachten also Schmerz und Verderben
Selbst über ewige Götter.
Und die armen Götter, oben am Himmel
Wandeln sie, qualvoll,
Trostlos unendliche Bahnen,
Und können nicht sterben,
Und schleppen mit sich
Ihr strahlendes Elend.

Ich aber, der Mensch,
Der niedriggepflanzte, der todbeglückte,
Ich klage nicht länger.

With her orphaned star-children
Shining in silent misery,
While love-lorn girls and tender poets
Dedicate to her their songs and tears.
Gentle moon! With a woman's heart
She still loves her lovely man.
As evening falls, she peeps out,
Pale and trembling, from a wisp of cloud,
And seeing her deserting spouse,
Wants in her anguish to call out: "Come!
Come! The children long for you –"
But at the sight of his wife
The defiant sun god glows
Deep purple
In rage and pain,
And hurries down, implacable,
To his cool and watery widower's bed.

Wicked hissing tongues
Thus brought pain and ruin
Even to the immortal gods.
And the wretched gods in the heavens
Wander tormented and disconsolate
In their endless orbits,
And cannot die,
Dragging with them
Their glittering pain.

But I, a human being,
Bound to lowly earth and blessed with death,
Will complain no more.

DIE NACHT AM STRANDE

Sternlos und kalt ist die Nacht,
Es gärt das Meer;
Und über dem Meer, platt auf dem Bauch,
Liegt der ungestalte Nordwind,
Und heimlich, mit ächzend gedämpfter Stimme,
Wie'n störriger Griesgram, der gutgelaunt wird,
Schwatzt er ins Wasser hinein,
Und erzählt viel tolle Geschichten,
Riesenmärchen, totschlaglaunig,
Uralte Sagen aus Norweg,
Und dazwischen, weitschallend, lacht er und heult er
Beschwörungslieder der Edda,
Auch Runensprüche,
So dunkeltrotzig und zaubergewaltig,
Daß die weißen Meerkinder
Hoch aufspringen und jauchzen,
Übermutberauscht.

Derweilen, am flachen Gestade,
Über den flutbefeuchteten Sand,
Schreitet ein Fremdling, mit einem Herzen,
Das wilder noch als Wind und Wellen.
Wo er hintritt,
Sprühen Funken und knistern die Muscheln;
Und er hüllt sich fest in den grauen Mantel,
Und schreitet rasch durch die wehende Nacht;-
Sicher geleitet vom kleinen Lichte,
Das lockend und lieblich schimmert
Aus einsamer Fischerhütte.

NIGHT ON THE SHORE

*Here the mythic dimension is Nordic, at least initially, but Heine
is less concerned with invoking particular myths than with a play
of the imagination across boundaries between everyday experience
and the stories we tell to try to make sense of it.*

On this cold and starless night,
The ocean seethes,
And over the sea, flat on its belly
Lies the rough north wind;
And quietly, with a muffled groaning voice,
Like a stubborn old codger for once in a good mood,
He chatters to the water
And tells mad stories,
Tales of giants in a mood for murder,
From ancient Nordic sagas,
But then he'll laugh and yell out loud
Magic incantations from the Edda,
And old runic sayings
So darkly defiant and spell-binding
That the white children of the sea
Rear up and shout with joy,
Drunk with high spirits.

Meanwhile, at the shore's edge
On the sea-soaked sand,
A stranger strides, with a heart
That's wilder still than wind or waves.
With every step
Sparks fly and sea-shells crunch;
He's wrapped up tight in his grey cloak
And hurries on through the blowy night,
Safely guided by the faint light
That glimmers, inviting and warm,
In the lonely fisherman's hut.

Vater und Bruder sind auf der See,
Und mutterseelenallein blieb dort
In der Hütte die Fischertochter,
Die wunderschöne Fischertochter.

Am Herde sitzt sie,
Und horcht auf des Wasserkessels
Ahnungssüßes, heimliches Summen,
Und schüttet knisterndes Reisig ins Feuer,
Und bläst hinein,
Da die flackernd roten Lichter
Zauberlieblich widerstrahlen
Auf das blühende Antlitz,
Auf die zarte, weiße Schulter,
Die rührend hervorlauscht
Aus dem groben, grauen Hemde,
Und auf die kleine, sorgsame Hand,
Die das Unterröckchen fester bindet
Um die feine Hüfte.

*

Aber plötzlich, die Tür springt auf,
Und es tritt herein der nächtige Fremdling;
Liebesicher ruht sein Auge
Auf dem weißen, schlanken Mädchen,
Das schauernd vor ihm steht,
Gleich einer erschrockenen Lilie;
Und er wirft den Mantel zur Erde,
Und lacht und spricht:
Siehst du, mein Kind, ich halte Wort,
Und ich komme, und mit mir kommt
Die alte Zeit, wo die Götter des Himmels
Niederstiegen zu Töchtern der Menschen,
Und die Töchter der Menschen umarmten,
Und mit ihnen zeugten
Zeptertragende Königsgeschlechter
Und Helden, Wunder der Welt.
Doch staune, mein Kind, nicht länger
Ob meiner Göttlichkeit,
Und, ich bitte dich, koche mir Tee mit Rum,

Father and brother are out at sea,
While motherless and alone in the hut
The fisherman's daughter is left,
The lovely fisherman's daughter.
She sits at the hearth
Listening to the kettle's
Cosy beckoning hum;
She throws kindling on the crackling fire
And blows on it
So that the flickering red light
Sheds a magical glow
On her fresh young face,
On her pale delicate shoulder,
Showing touchingly bare
From her rough grey shift,
And on her small neat hand
Which gathers her skirt more tightly
Around her slender hips.

*

But suddenly the door bursts open and
In comes the nocturnal stranger;
Sure in his love, his eye rests
On the pale thin girl
Who sits before him shivering
Like a frightened lily,
And he throws down his cloak
And says with a laugh:
You see, my child, I kept my word;
I have come and with me has come
The ancient time when the gods in heaven
Descended to the daughters of mortals
And embraced the daughters of mortals,
And with them produced
Sceptre-bearing generations of kings
And heroes, astounding to the world.
But be amazed no longer, my child,
At my godliness;
I beg you make me tea with rum,

Denn draußen wars kalt,
Und bei solcher Nachtluft
Frieren auch wir, wir ewigen Götter,
Und kriegen wir leicht den göttlichsten Schnupfen,
Und einen unsterblichen Husten.

ERKLÄRUNG

Herangedämmert kam der Abend,
Wilder toste die Flut,
Und ich saß am Strand, und schaute zu
Dem weißen Tanz der Wellen,
Und meine Brust schwoll auf wie das Meer,
Und sehnend ergriff mich ein tiefes Heimweh
Nach dir, du holdes Bild,
Das überall mich umschwebt,
Und überall mich ruft,
Überall, überall,
Im Sausen des Windes, im Brausen des Meers,
Und im Seufzen der eigenen Brust.

Mit leichtem Rohr schrieb ich in den Sand:
"Agnes, ich liebe Dich!"
Doch böse Wellen ergossen sich
Über das süße Bekenntnis,
Und löschten es aus.
Zerbrechliches Rohr, zerstiebender Sand,
Zerfließende Wellen, euch trau ich nicht mehr!
Der Himmel wird dunkler, mein Herz wird wilder,
Und mit starker Hand, aus Norwegs Wäldern,
Reiß ich die höchste Tanne

For it was cold outside
And in such night air
Even we eternal gods will freeze
And easily catch the divinest of colds
And immortal coughs.

DECLARATION

*From direct perception of a scene by the shore, emotion soon
pushes the poet beyond the present moment into the realm of
wishful fantasy. In doing so, Heine pushes the Romantic impulse
to melodramatic heights but in the very excess there is a knowing
and joyful self-indulgence.*

With evening, darkness fell,
The sea raged wild,
And I sat on the shore and watched
The white dance of the waves.
My breast swelled like the sea
And I was gripped by a deep longing
For you, a vision of loveliness,
That floats everywhere around me,
And calls me everywhere,
Everywhere, everywhere –
In the howling of the wind, the roaring of the sea,
And the sighing of my own breast.

With a thin reed I wrote in the sand:
"Agnes, I love you!"
But the cruel waves gushed over
My sweet confession
And wiped it out.
Weak reed, shifting sand,
Dissolving waves – I trust you no more!
The sky grows darker, my heart grows wilder,
And I seize the tallest pine
From the Norwegian woods with one mighty hand

Und tauche sie ein
In des Ätnas glühenden Schlund, und mit solcher
Feuergetränkten Riesenfeder
Schrieb ich an die dunkle Himmelsdecke:
"Agnes, ich liebe Dich!"

Jedwede Nacht lodert alsdann
Dort oben die ewige Flammenschrift,
Und alle nachwachsende Enkelgeschlechter
Lesen jauchzend die Himmelsworte:
"Agnes, ich liebe Dich!"

FRAGEN

Am Meer, am wüsten, nächtlichen Meer
Steht ein Jüngling-Mann,
Die Brust voll Wehmut, das Haupt voll Zweifel,
Und mit düstern Lippen fragt er die Wogen:

"O löst mir das Rätsel des Lebens,
Das qualvoll uralte Rätsel,
Worüber schon manche Häupter gegrübelt,
Häupter in Hieroglyphenmützen,
Häupter in Turban und schwarzem Barett,
Perückenhäupter und tausend andre
Arme, schwitzende Menschenhäupter –
Sagt mir, was bedeutet der Mensch?
Woher ist er kommen? Wo geht er hin?
Wer wohnt dort oben auf goldenen Sternen?

Es murmeln die Wogen ihr ew'ges Gemurmel,
Es wehet der Wind, es fliehen die Wolken,
Es blinken die Sterne, gleichgültig und kalt,
Und ein Narr wartet auf Antwort.

And plunge it in
To Etna's glowing crater, and with this
Fire-soaked gigantic pen
I write on the darkening canopy of the heavens:
"Agnes, I love you!"

Each and every night from then
The eternal flaming script blazes up there,
And all the coming generations of children
Will shout with joy to read the heavenly words:
"Agnes, I love you!"

QUESTIONS

This time Heine observes the emotions aroused by the sea from the outside, putting the questions in the mouth of a third person. In the face of the young man's questions, nature remains eloquently mute.

By the sea, the desolate night-dark sea,
Stands a young man,
His heart full of sorrow, his head full of doubt,
And with mournful lips he asks the waves:

"O solve me the riddle of life,
That ancient tormenting riddle
So many heads have wrestled with –
Heads in wizards' hats,
Heads in turbans and black skull-caps,
Heads in wigs and a thousand other
Wretched perspiring human heads –
Tell me what mankind means;
Where does he come from? Where is he going?
Who lives up there among the golden stars?"

The waves they murmur their eternal murmur,
The wind blows, the clouds race,
The stars twinkle, indifferent and cold,
And a fool waits for an answer.

STURM

Es wütet der Sturm,
Und er peitscht die Wellen,
Und die Well'n, wutschäumend und bäumend,
Türmen sich auf, und es wogen lebendig
Die weißen Wasserberge,
Und das Schifflein erklimmt sie,
Hastig mühsam,
Und plötzlich stürzt es hinab
In schwarze, weitgähnende Flutabgründe –

O Meer!
Mutter der Schönheit, der Schaumentstiegenen!
Großmutter der Liebe! schone meiner!
Schon flattert, leichenwitternd,
Die weiße, gespenstische Möwe,
Und wetzt an dem Mastbaum den Schnabel,
Und lechzt, voll Fraßbegier, nach dem Herzen,
Das vom Ruhm deiner Tochter ertönt,
Und das dein Enkel, der kleine Schalk,
Zum Spielzeug erwählt.

Vergebens mein Bitten und Flehn!
Mein Rufen verhallt im tosenden Sturm,
Im Schlachtlärm der Winde.
Es braust und pfeift und prasselt und heult,
Wie ein Tollhaus von Tönen!

Und zwischendurch hör ich vernehmbar
Lockende Harfenlaute,
Sehnsuchtwilden Gesang,
Seelenschmelzend und seelenzerreißend,
Und ich erkenne die Stimme.

STORM

Now at sea in all senses of the term, Heine's storm is on the inside as well as the outside. Again he draws on a mixture of sources, in this instance the Greek myth of Venus's generation from the sea, coupled with the contemporary enthusiasm for Scotland as a source for the Romantic imagination.

The tempest rages,
Whipping the waves,
And the foaming waves rear up in fury,
Piling high, making living
Mountains of white water;
And the little ship clambers up,
Struggling to the top,
Only to plunge back down
Into black, yawning chasms of water.

Oh sea!
Mother of Venus who rose from the foam,
Grandmother of Cupid! Spare me!
Already the ghostly white seabird
Flaps around us, sensing death,
And sharpens its bill against the mast,
Greedy for the taste of my heart,
Which resounds with praise of your daughter,
And which your grandson, the little scoundrel,
Has chosen for a plaything.

In vain my prayers and entreaties!
My cries are lost in the raging storm,
In the noisy war of winds.
There's a roaring, whistling, rattling and howling,
A sheer madhouse of sounds!

And through the tumult I can hear
The bewitching sound of the harp,
And wild songs of yearning
Which melt the soul and tear it to shreds –
And I know the voice.

Fern an schottischer Felsenküste,
Wo das graue Schlößlein hinausragt
Über die brandende See,
Dort, am hochgewölbten Fenster,
Steht eine schöne, kranke Frau,
Zartdurchsichtig und marmorblaß,
Und sie spielt die Harfe und singt,
Und der Wind durchwühlt ihre langen Locken,
Und trägt ihr dunkles Lied
Über das weite, stürmende Meer.

MEERESSTILLE

Meeresstille! Ihre Strahlen
Wirft die Sonne auf das Wasser,
Und im wogenden Geschmeide
Zieht das Schiff die grünen Furchen.

Bei dem Steuer liegt der Bootsmann
Auf dem Bauch, und schnarchet leise.
Bei dem Mastbaum, segelflickend,
Kauert der beteerte Schiffsjung.

Hinterm Schmutze seiner Wangen
Sprüht es rot, wehmütig zuckt es
Um das breite Maul, und schmerzlich
Schaun die großen, schönen Augen.

Denn der Kapitän steht vor ihm,
Tobt und flucht und schilt ihn: Spitzbub.
"Spitzbub! Einen Hering hast du
Aus der Tonne mir gestohlen!"

Far away on the rocky Scottish coast
Where a grey castle juts out
Over the boiling sea,
There at a high-arched window
Stands a lovely, sickly woman,
Her delicate skin as pale as marble,
And she plays the harp and sings,
The wind runs through her long hair,
And carries her dark song
Over the wide stormy sea.

CALM SEA

Heine at his most darkly playful. The action is all in the here and now, the scenes sharply observed, unmediated by myth or memory.

Calm sea! The sun
Casts its rays upon the water
And through the jewelled waves
The ship ploughs green furrows.

By the helm lies the bosun
On his belly, snoring gently.
At the mast, mending sails,
Crouches the tar-stained ship's boy.

Behind the dirt on his cheeks,
His skin's inflamed, there's grief in the grimace
Of his wide mouth, and pain
In his big beautiful eyes.

For the captain stands over him,
Raging, cursing, and calling him scoundrel:
"Scoundrel! You've stolen a herring
Out of the barrel."

Meeresstille! Aus den Wellen
Taucht hervor ein kluges Fischlein,
Wärmt das Köpfchen in der Sonne,
Plätschert lustig mit dem Schwänchen.

Doch die Möwe, aus den Lüften,
Schießt herunter auf das Fischlein,
Und den raschen Raub im Schnabel,
Schwingt sie sich hinauf ins Blaue.

SEEGESPENST

Ich aber lag am Rande des Schiffes,
Und schaute, träumenden Auges,
Hinab in das spiegelklare Wasser,
Und schaute tiefer und tiefer –
Bis tief, im Meeresgrunde,
Anfangs wie dämmernde Nebel,
Jedoch allmählich farbenbestimmter,
Kirchenkuppel und Türme sich zeigten,
Und endlich, sonnenklar, eine ganze Stadt,
Altertümlich niederländisch,
Und menschenbelebt.
Bedächtige Männer, schwarzbemäntelt,
Mit weißen Halskrausen und Ehrenketten
Und langen Degen und langen Gesichtern,
Schreiten, über den wimmelden Marktplatz,
Nach dem treppenhohen Rathaus,
Wo steinerne Kaiserbilder
Wacht halten mit Zepter und Schwert.
Unferne, vor langen Häuserreihn,
Wo spiegelblanke Fenster

Calm sea! Out of the waves
Peeps a smart little fish,
Warms his head in the sun
And splashes in fun with his tail.

But a gull, swooping down
On the fish from the heights
Grabs him up in his beak
And sweeps back up in a flash.

SEA SPECTRE

*Probably Heine's best-known puncturing of the Romantic
sensibility. The journey of the poet's imagination in this poem
mirrors the larger rhythm of the sequence but leaves open the
question of whether or how he can recover from his 'madness'.*

But I was lying at the rail of the ship,
Looking down with dreamy eyes
Into the crystal-clear water,
Then deeper and deeper I looked,
Till deep down on the seabed,
At first dim and cloudy
Then gradually sharper and clearer,
Appeared church steeples and towers
And then, clear as daylight, a whole town,
Ancient and Dutch,
Teeming with people.
Grave gentlemen dressed in black
With white ruffs and chains of office,
Long swords and long faces,
Stride through the crowded market-place
To the townhall steps
Where stone images of emperors
Stand watch with sceptre and sword.
Nearby, past long rows of houses
With mirror-bright windows

Und pyramidisch beschnittene Linden,
Wandeln seidenrauschende Jungfern,
Schlanke Leibchen, die Blumengesichter
Sittsam umschlossen von schwarzen Mützchen
Und hervorquellendem Goldhaar.
Bunte Gesellen, in spanischer Tracht,
Stolzieren vorüber und nicken.
Bejahrte Frauen,
In braunen, verschollnen Gewändern,
Gesangbuch und Rosenkranz in der Hand,
Eilen, trippelnden Schritts,
Nach dem großen Dome,
Getrieben von Glockenläute
Und rauschendem Orgelton.

Mich selbst ergreift des fernen Klangs
Geheimnisvoller Schauer!
Unendliches Sehnen, tiefe Wehmut
Beschleicht mein Herz,
Mein kaum geheiltes Herz;-
Mir ist, als würden seine Wunden
Von lieben Lippen aufgeküßt,
Und täten wieder bluten –
Heiße rote Tropfen,
Die lang und langsam niederfalln
Auf ein altes Haus, dort unten
In der tiefen Meerstadt,
Auf ein altes, hochgegiebeltes Haus,
Das melancholisch menschenleer ist,
Nur daß am untern Fenster
Ein Mädchen sitzt,
Den Kopf auf den Arm gestützt,
Wie ein armes, vergessenes Kind –
Und ich kenne dich armes, vergessenes Kind!

So tief, meertief also
Verstecktest du dich vor mir,
Aus kindischer Laune,

And pyramid-shaped linden trees,
Young women saunter in rustling silks,
Slim of body, their faces like flowers,
Wearing modest black bonnets
Over long golden tresses.
Young men in motley Spanish garb
Strut past and nod their greetings.
Older women
Clad in old-fashioned brown,
Carrying hymn-books and rosaries,
Hurry along with stumbling steps
To the great cathedral,
Urged on by the peal of bells
And the swelling sound of the organ.

The far off sounds fill me
With a mysterious dread!
Endless longing, deep sorrow
Seize my heart,
My scarcely recovered heart:-
It's as though its wounds
Were being kissed by those dear lips
And made to bleed again –
Hot red drops
Falling long and slow
To an old gabled house down there,
Sadly empty of human life,
Except that, at a lower window,
A young girl sits,
Her head resting on her arm
Like a poor lost child –
And I know you, poor lost child!

So deep, sea deep indeed,
You hid yourself from me
Out of a childish whim,

Und konntest nicht mehr herauf,
Und saßest fremd unter fremden Leuten,
Jahrhundertlang,
Derweilen ich, die Seele voll Gram,
Auf der ganzen Erde dich suchte,
Und immer dich suchte,
Du Immergeliebte,
Du Längstverlorene,
Du Endlichgefundene –
Ich hab dich gefunden und schaue wieder
Dein süßes Gesicht,
Die klugen, treuen Augen,
Das liebe Lächeln –
Und nimmer will ich dich wieder verlassen,
Und ich komme hinab zu dir,
Und mit ausgebreiteten Armen
Stürz ich hinab an dein Herz –

Aber zur rechten Zeit noch
Ergriff mich beim Fuß der Kapitän,
Und zog mich vom Schiffsrand,
Und rief, ärgerlich lachend:
Doktor, sind Sie des Teufels?

REINIGUNG

Bleib du in deiner Meerestiefe,
Wahnsinniger Traum,
Der du einst so manche Nacht
Mein Herz mit falschem Glück gequält hast,
Und jetzt, als Seegespenst,
Sogar am hellen Tag mich bedrohest –

No longer able to surface,
But lived as a stranger among strangers
For centuries.
Meanwhile, with my heart full of grief,
I searched the whole world for you,
searched for you always,
Eternal beloved,
Long lost,
Found at last –
I have found you and see again
Your sweet face,
Your wise trusting eyes,
Your dear smile –
Never more will I leave you,
And I'm coming down to you,
And with arms stretched wide
I'll plunge down to your heart –

But just in time
The captain seized me by the foot
And pulled me back from the rail,
Crying out with a vexed laugh:
Doctor, are you mad?

PURIFICATION

*The poet recovers his equilibrium as the breeze sets in and the ship
makes sail, cleansing body and soul. Heine beautifully captures
the lift and surge of a vessel, along with the spirits of its crew, as
the wind catches the sails.*

Stay down in your ocean depths,
Insane dream
Which for so many nights has
Tortured me with deceptive happiness,
And now, as a sea spectre,
Threatens me even in broad daylight.

Bleib du dort unten, in Ewigkeit,
Und ich werfe noch zu dir hinab
All meine Schmerzen und Sünden,
Und die Schellenkappe der Torheit,
Die so lange mein Haupt umklingelt,
Und die kalte, gleißende Schlangenhaut
Der Heuchelei,
Die mir so lang die Seele umwunden,
Die kranke Seele,
Die gottverleugnende, engelverleugnende,
Unselige Seele –
Hoiho! Hoiho! Da kommt der Wind!
Die Segel auf! Sie flattern und schwell'n!
Über die stillverderbliche Fläche
Eilet das Schiff,
Und es jauchzt die befreite Seele.

IM HAFEN

Glücklich der Mann, der den Hafen erreicht hat,
Und hinter sich ließ das Meer und die Stürme,
Und jetzo warm und ruhig sitzt
Im guten Ratskeller zu Bremen.

Wie doch die Welt so traulich und lieblich
In Römerglas sich widerspiegelt,
Und wie der wogende Mikrokosmus
Sonnig hinabfließt ins durstige Herz!
Alles erblick ich im Glas,
Alte und neue Völkergeschichte,
Türken und Griechen, Hegel und Gans,
Zitronenwälder und Wachtparaden,

Stay down there for eternity
And I'll throw you down
All my sorrows and sins,
And this fool's cap-and-bells of madness
That so long have tinkled round my head,
And the cold slippery snakeskin
Of hypocrisy
That for so long has enveloped my soul,
My sickly soul,
My god-denying, angel-denying
Benighted soul –
Hoho! Hoho! Here comes the breeze!
Up with the sails! They flap and fill!
Over the calm but ever-shifting surface of the sea
The ship surges on,
And my unshackled soul cries out for joy.

IN PORT

The poet toasts his return to port with a promiscuous and satirical use of cultural and religious sources, including Hegel's 'world-spirit' (and that of his disciple Gans), which unsurprisingly mirrors his own rapturous inebriated state.

Happy the man who's arrived in port
And left behind the sea and the storms,
And now sits snug and warm
In the town hall cellar in Bremen.

How familiar and warm is the world
Mirrored in your drinking glass
When it slips in microcosm happily down
To your thirsty heart!
I see everything in the glass,
The history of peoples ancient and new,
Turks and Greeks, Hegel and Gans,
Lemon groves and guards' parades,

Berlin und Schilda und Tunis und Hamburg,
Vor allem aber das Bild der Geliebten,
Das Engelköpfchen auf Rheinweingoldgrund.

O, wie schön! Wie schön bist du, Geliebte!
Du bist wie eine Rose!
Nicht wie die Rose von Schiras,
Die hafizbesungene Nachtigallbraut;
Nicht wie die Rose von Saron,
Die heiligrote, prophetengefeierte;-
Du bist wie die Ros' im Ratskeller zu Bremen!
Das ist die Rose der Rosen,
Je älter sie wird, je lieblicher blüht sie,
Und ihr himmlischer Duft, er hat mich beseligt,
Er hat mich begeistert, er hat mich berauscht,
Und hielt mich nicht fest, am Schopfe fest,
Der Ratskellermeister von Bremen,
Ich wäre gepurzelt!

Der brave Mann! Wir saßen beisammen
Und tranken wie Brüder,
Wir sprachen von hohen, heimlichen Dingen,
Wir seufzten und sanken uns in die Arme,
Und er hat mich bekehrt zum Glauben der Liebe –
Ich trank auf das Wohl meiner bittersten Feinde,
Und allen schlechten Poeten vergab ich,
Wie einst mir selber vergeben soll werden –
Ich weinte vor Andacht, und endlich
Erschlossen sich mir die Pforten des Heils,
Wo die zwölf Apostel, die heilgen Stückfässer,
Schweigend pred'gen, und doch so verständlich
Für alle Völker.

Das sind Männer!
Unscheinbar von außen, in hölzernen Röcklein,
Sind sie von innen schöner und leuchtender
Denn all die stolzen Leviten des Tempels
Und des Herodes Trabanten und Höflinge,

Berlin and Schilda and Tunis and Hamburg,
Most of all the image of my beloved,
Her angelic head against a Rhine-wine golden background.

O how lovely. How beautiful you are, my love!
You are like a rose!
Not like the rose of Shiraz,
The nightingale bride praised in the song by Hafiz,
Not like the rose of Sharon,
The sacred red rose, celebrated by prophets:-
You are like the rose in the town cellar in Bremen!
That is the rose of roses –
The older it grows, the fairer it blooms,
And its heavenly scent has blessed me,
Has inspired me, put me in raptures,
And had not the cellar master in Bremen
Held me fast by the scruff of the neck
I'd have tumbled head over heels!

That fine fellow! We sat together
And drank like brothers,
We talked of lofty mysterious things,
We sighed and fell into each other's arms,
And he restored my faith in love –
I drank the health of my bitterest foes,
And I forgave all bad poets,
As I some day should be forgiven.
I wept from sheer piety and in the end
The gates of salvation opened before me,
Where the twelve apostles, holy wine-casks all,
Preach in silence, and yet with meaning
For all people.

What men!
Insignificant from outside in their clumsy garb,
Inside they are more bright and beautiful
Than all the proud Levites of the temple
And Herod's courtiers and hangers-on,

Die goldgeschmückten, die purpurgekleideten –
Hab ich doch immer gesagt,
Nicht unter ganz gemeinen Leuten,
Nein, in der allerbesten Gesellschaft,
Lebte beständig der König des Himmels!

Hallelujah! Wie lieblich umwehen mich
Die Palmen von Beth El!
Wie duften die Myrrhen von Hebron!
Wie rauscht der Jordan und taumelt vor Freude!-
Auch meine unsterbliche Seele taumelt,
Und ich taumle mit ihr, und taumelnd
Bringt mich die Treppe hinauf, ans Tagslicht,
Der brave Ratskellermeister von Bremen.

Du braver Ratskellermeister von Bremen!
Siehst du, auf den Dächern der Häuser sitzen
Die Engel und sind betrunken und singen;
Die glühende Sonne dort oben
Ist nur eine rote, betrunkene Nase,
Die Nase des Weltgeists;
Und um die rote Weltgeistnase
Dreht sich die ganze, betrunkene Welt.

All bejewelled in gold and clad in purple –
Haven't I always said
That it's not among the common people
But in the very best society
That the King of Heaven made his home!

Hallelujah! How wonderfully
The palms of Beth El blow round me!
How fragrant the myrrh of Hebron!
How joyful the rushing reeling waters of the Jordan!
And my undying soul also reels,
And I reel with it, and reeling
I am lifted up the stairway to daylight
By the worthy cellar master of Bremen!

Worthy cellar master from Bremen!
Look! There on the roofs of the houses
Sit angels, drunkenly singing;
The glowing sun up there
Is only a red drunken nose,
The nose of the world-spirit;
And around the world-spirit's red nose
Circles the whole drunken world.

EPILOG

Wie auf dem Felde die Weizenhalmen,
So wachsen und wogen im Menschengeist
Die Gedanken.
Aber die zarten Gedanken der Liebe
Sind wie lustig dazwischenblühende,
Rot' und blaue Blumen!

Rot' und blaue Blumen!
Der mürrische Schnitter verwirft euch als nutzlos,
Hölzerne Flegel zerdreschen euch höhnend,
Sogar der hablose Wanderer,
Den eu'r Anblick ergötzt und erquickt,
Schüttelt das Haupt,
Und nennt euch schönes Unkraut.
Aber die ländliche Jungfrau,
Die Kränzewinderin,
Verehrt euch und pflückt euch,
Und schmückt mit euch die schönen Locken,
Und also geziert, eilt sie zum Tanzplatz,
Wo Pfeifen und Geigen lieblich ertönen,
Oder zur stillen Buche,
Wo die Stimme des Liebsten noch lieblicher tönt
Als Pfeifen und Geigen.

EPILOGUE

Back on dry land and now well inland, the sequence ends in a tranquil pastoral mood, the surging disordered emotions of the sea left far behind.

Just as wheat stalks grow in the field,
So do thoughts ripen and sway
In the mind of man.
But tender thoughts of love
Are like the red and blue flowers
Gaily blooming in between.

Red and blue flowers!
The sullen reaper rejects you as useless;
Wooden flails cut you down in scorn,
Even the hapless wanderer,
Who is delighted and refreshed by the sight of you,
Shakes his head
And calls you beautiful weeds.
But the country girl,
Weaver of garlands,
Adores you and plucks you
To adorn her lovely tresses,
And thus tricked out, she hurries to the village dance,
Where pipes and fiddles play lovely music,
Or she goes to the quiet beech tree
Where her beloved's voice sounds yet more lovely
Than pipes and fiddles.

HEINRICH HEINE was a leading poet and author of diverse prose works in the generation following Goethe and Schiller. His writings range from lyrical poetry in a Romantic vein to works of biting satire. He was born in Düsseldorf in 1797 and died in Paris in 1856, where for twenty-five years he had lived in exile from his native Germany. His move reflected his attraction to the revolutionary ideas of France and also the struggle for a writer of his political stripe to flourish in Germany. His *Buch der Lieder* (Book of Songs, 1827) remains among the most widely read of all German books of poetry. His numerous prose works included autobiography, literary criticism, political and cultural commentary. In the last eight years of his life he was confined to bed with a debilitating illness, through which, however, he continued to write and comment on public events

RICHARD CROCKATT was born in Scotland in 1947 and lives in North Norfolk with his wife Julia who is a photographer. He studied English Literature and German at the University of Edinburgh after which he spent two years in Germany working as an English teacher and translator.

On his return to the UK he moved into the field of history and entered an academic career, retiring from the University of East Anglia in 2011 as Professor of American History. Among his publications was *The Fifty Years War: The United States and the Soviet Union in World Politics, 1941-1991* (Routledge, 1995). In retirement he has returned to his German interests, both historical and literary, of which these Heine translations are fruit. On the historical front he has published *Einstein and Twentieth Century Politics* (Oxford University Press, 2016).